I0267920

The Moment and the Sequence

poems by

Edward D. Miller

Finishing Line Press
Georgetown, Kentucky

The Moment
and the Sequence

Copyright © 2021 by Edward D. Miller
ISBN 978-1-64662-501-7 First Edition
All rights reserved under International and Pan-American Copyright Conventions. No part of this book may be reproduced in any manner whatsoever without written permission from the publisher, except in the case of brief quotations embodied in critical articles and reviews.

ACKNOWLEDGMENTS

It is with gratitude that the author would like to acknowledge the following publications in which these poems first appeared:

The Bangalore Review ~ "The House That Lota de Soares Macedo Built in Samambaia";
Drunk Monkeys ~ "Express Mail", and "Pre-existing Soliloquy";
Crack the Spine ~ "Yesterday I Had the Hiccups";
The Wilderness House Literary Review ~ "President Obama is in Town for the General Assembly" (the poem's title has been updated);
Coldnoon: International Journal of Travel Writing & Travelling Cultures ~ "The Triumvirate", "The Trade Minister", "Two Coins and Three Stanzas", "La voix de ma mère", and "Dancing on the Ship of Theseus";
Bluing the Blade ~ "Call Me Surely";
Griffel ~ "The Warning" (published as "The Argument");
The Write Launch ~ "The Moment and the Sequence", "To Tell the Truth", and "Binge-Watching a Dream."

Publisher: Leah Huete de Maines
Editor: Christen Kincaid
Cover Art: Depositphotos
Author Photo: Stephanie Berger
Cover Design: Elizabeth Maines McCleavy

Order online: www.finishinglinepress.com
also available on amazon.com

Author inquiries and mail orders:
Finishing Line Press
PO Box 1626
Georgetown, Kentucky 40324
USA

Table of Contents

To Tell the Truth 1

Binge-Watching a Dream 4

This Flawed Container 6

Dancing on the Ship of Theseus 8

La voix de ma mère 10

Call Me Surely 12

The Trade Minister 14

President Obama is in Town for the General Assembly 16

Pre-existing Soliloquy 17

Express Mail 18

The House That Lota De Macedo Soares Built In Samambaia 20

The Triumvirate 22

Rumi's Stipend 23

The Warning 24

Two Coins and Three Stanzas 26

The Moment and the Sequence 28

Yesterday I Had the Hiccups 30

For Ray

To Tell the Truth

Colin spoke in aphorisms
as if he had the burden
and the insight of a previous life.
Dialogue didn't interest him much at all;
instead the duty to present life
qua soliloquy took centerstage.
But he did notice details
about a listener's posture and gesture:
after all, a performer studies the spectator.
Once he said of a high-minded school-mate
we both disliked
there's a fine line
between martyrdom and masochism.
He added:
"and why can't he just sit still for god's sake?"

I took pride in having a friend
whose hero was Blaise Pascal
He had memorized quite a few of the Pensées.
His favorite:
*Tout le malheur des hommes vient d'une seule
chose, qui est de ne savoir pas demeurer en repos,
dans une chambre.*
I suspected he liked me
because I loved Chico Marx.
He went to the Everyman Cinema
for the yearly Marx Bros. festival
as if it was returning to a homeland.
He argued that *A Night of the Opera*
was their best film,
though as an English kid
he had no idea that Kitty Carlisle
went on to feature in the game show
To Tell the Truth.
He could repeat every line of Groucho's
from the cabin scene.

He took me to his pub one day after walking home
from Highgate to Hampstead through the Heath
(by way of Keat's house of course)
as if he was letting me
into a locked room
of a dilapidated ancestral home.
Inside the nicotine-stained inner sanctum:
an unlikely mix of working men,
young bohemians on the dole
pretending to be working class,
and older gay men with posh accents
all beyond tipsy by mid-afternoon.
A few chain-smoking women
with ashy laughs singed by COPD
acted as the chorus
to the drama of tragic masculinity.
Everyone appeared to await
Colin's chronic coughing wit
that was sure to emerge after his third pint.
How could someone so young
spit out words so wise
and as bitter as the ale he drank.
Afterward, stumbling up Finchley Road
to get onion bhajis
he grumbled about his pub friends,
"they wouldn't piss on me
if I was burning in a fire."

Somehow that comforted him
for Colin distrusted sentiment.
One afternoon I found out he could do card tricks
and practiced in the mirror
of his Frognal Lane bedroom for hours.
He planned to sit for the Oxbridge Exam
and was no doubt destined for Cambridge
just like his nemesis, the masochistic martyr.

Another afternoon much later
I realized his family was Jewish
from a rather ornate heirloom-y menorah
in the unused dining room
although he knew from day one
that my father was a Brooklyn-born Jew
now living in Brookline, Massachusetts.
My American-ness
was far more interesting to him,
and that I had seen *Taxi Driver* twice already
and could mimic Robert DeNiro as Travis Bickle
repeating "you talkin' to me" in the mirror.

Also, Colin was impressed that I could sing
the lyrics that Groucho sang in the faux-anthem
of Fredonia from Duck Soup.
I still can:
"The last man nearly ruined this place,
He didn't know what to do with it.
If you think this country's bad off now,
Just wait 'til I get through with it."
I'd try to google Colin now to find him
but to tell the truth
I just can't remember his last name.

Binge-Watching a Dream

When he awakens, the dream tucks itself in.
At bedtime, the dream starts the night shift.
And so
Inside the lazy contraction of slumber
Is an energetic stretch.
And so
He falls into an action-packed reverie that is
Kinda like a first-person shooter video game
Except that all the characters are familiar to him
Even though they are more muscular
And have perfect hair.
Behind the cartoonish blood
And the bubblegum guns,
The dream has a not so subtle message
Spoken in a baritone voice, source unseen:
You may win. You may lose.
But either way
You survive.
During the day,
The dream hibernates
At the edge of her awareness.
The dream snores, getting louder
As her head slumps into the afternoon.
And so,
It is kinda like an impatient car
Eager to make a left turn
Onto Route 6 in August.
And so,
It accelerates like it decided
To make the light toward Truro.
Remarkably the dream reaches the center
Of her catnap in no time at all.
As it if is trapped inside
Chequessett Chocolate with lotsa money. Maybe.
And this is what the dream instructs:
You may win. You may lose.

But either way
You survive.
The dream yearns to take a vacation
Away from the cave of consciousness.
And so
Why should it be trapped inside
Kinda like a coalminer chipping away
At a walled-in psyche
But doomed to repeat?
And so
It couldn't go away
To some imaginary cumulous cloud until later.
An activity proclaims its importance:
To tell the story again and again,
With a new glitch each time. Maybe.
But no matter how shambolic
The dream becomes
The message intervenes:
You may win. You may lose.
But either way
You survive.

This Flawed Container

I know you could forget people entirely
if they just weren't everywhere:
smelly, unpleasant to look at, shrill,
with sandpaper as skin.
If only they were a rumor
rather than an in-your-face actuality;
a nuisance that one could protect oneself
from by applying repellent.
(I read that rose geranium oil rebuffs ticks.)

I agree with you:
Misanthropy itself may spit, but it becalms the air
like fine perfume.
Nihilism fits like spandex but breathes like linen.

I get it:
You used to blame power
and varied ideological state apparatuses.
Or the structure of the unjust economy.
Or bizarre patriarchal practices.
But now you realize that human beings
—from the individual to the crowd,
from the idea to its realization—
do not really qualify as a species.
Humanity is just a tired genre
And one should never sit there
and watch the predictable plot unfold.

I ask you:
What metric to measure one's displeasure?
Best to tend to own one's garden, after all.
Who knew Voltaire was so right?

My love:
If only we could mutate faster
into some other life form.
I'd be first in line to trade in this mortal coil
for a new model
Like you, I hope that our bodies
can be buried on the internet
so we don't pollute the earth
with our ash or flesh and bone.

Nonetheless, while here,
prisoner to this flawed container,
I'd like to marry you.

Dancing on the Ship of Theseus

One of the perfectly-postured matriarchs
In my family once said
He is just the sum of his contradictions
Could have been my Aunt
When Mother admitted
That Papa exasperated her
Or it could have been Mother
When she took that big sister tone
With my twice-divorced Auntie
Describing how men keep a secret residence
Down in the antipodes
While women remain up north
Now I use the equation to explain
My need to summer upon the heathered cliffs of
"Paradox Island"
A clue
You don't need to take a ferry
From the South Shore to get there
Just wriggle your nose like
Bewitched's suburban rebel Samantha
Or blink your eyes emphatically
Imitating pin-up-in-a-bottle Jeannie
As a child I believed women
Were either articulate or magical
Or both
I pretended to be a cry-baby so I could get a hug
Their men schlumped in black and white
And never gossiped
Instead they discussed politics or the "market"—How boring!
The women wore chunky turquoise jewelry
And bright batik sundresses
They let each other know they were listening
Through eye contact and slight nods
They only stopped talking
When they danced to Motown music
With hands floating above their heads

My hippie-ish cousin introduced me
To the word "oxymoron"
She just adored reciting Shakespeare
And knotting macramé
I loved to honk the horn in her red
Karmann Ghia sportscar with the top down
We darted through the smug lanes
Of Shelter Island Heights laughing
She took her vanity quite seriously
As if she pledged allegiance to purple bandanas
And tie-dyed t-shirts
She told me that
My mischief bordered on perfection itself

La voix de ma mère

I was born at the French Hospital,
between 29th and 30th streets
and 8th and 9th avenues.
La Société Française de Bienfaisance
built the building in 1928.
Now it is an apartment building,
designated as mixed income.
Babe Ruth died there.
It is also where Vito Corleone's
gunshot wound was treated.
Beth lived in a brownstone down the block
so later in life
I often walked past the French Apartments.
My mom chose its maternity ward
because it didn't separate the newborn
from the mother at birth,
the common practice in 1960.
Nonetheless I started to fear the end of the world
as soon as I acquired language.
This trepidation has returned.
It wakes me at 3:33 each morning.
My mother told me her
Irish grandma used to warn her about men:
"Fine words butter no parsnips."
But I say:
"Cursing a foe tastes as sweet as agave."
Just imagine the foul language I reserve
to describe the impostor in the White House.
Yes, it relieves tension
but those words embitter too soon.
My mother would warn me:
"Don't be driven mad
by an onslaught of patriarchal insanity."
And then she would add:
"and please remember to trim
your wandering eyebrow hairs!"

Even in her stern voice
there was a tinge and twinkle
of warmth and whimsy.
My mother's French professor in college
was the Belgian-born novelist
Marguerite Yourcenar.
Apparently, my mom didn't excel
in French literature.
Nevertheless "Madame" invited Mother
to visit her and Grace Frick
one summer on Mount Desert Island
off the coast of Maine.
My mother ended up in medical school.
Memoirs of Hadrian is one of my favorite novels.

Call Me Surely

If I told a story of he and I
what happens to the one about me and him?
Pronouns are *prêt-à-porter* not made to order.
Neither experience nor perspective
changes an object's mass.
Shall I upload consciousness
to a drone hovering above,
transmitting data *ad nauseum*?

How to remain faithful when the
words we use are as frisky
as 20-somethings high on early 90s ecstasy?
Name this, re-name that, discern categories,
withhold the bridge between.
I pay tax but I'm no taxonomist.

Predictably, I use a colon
and make a generalization:
each of us yearns to be interviewed live
as the victim of the broadcast itself.
If only we could have been left to our own devices
(even while our devices
seemingly yearn to mingle).
Surely pen(wo)manship
is as important as spelling.

I used to measure success
via the high-end accoutrements
I could give to my beloved.
How manipulative!
But surely the wrapping paper was not transactional.
I dreamed of a home away
from medicine and media, silly me.
But now I'm obsessed with the state of things,
and my perfect pitch has gone shrill
railing against authoritarianism.

GPS won't lead anyone
to a place where books
fall open to passages already underlined.
A place where we,
unforgivably old and yet frightfully adolescent,
could begin to unmoor from categories.
If only our vases were weary of wildflowers!
If only these bodies were free
of diagnoses and inexplicable ailments!
If only crayons and credibility could erase
the poppycock and wrongfulness of this regime.

The Trade Minister

Some say Trade Minister Tagomi
melted the ice
and flooded the creek.
But I doubt it.
If Tagomi was only a character
in Philip K. Dick's *The Man in the High Castle*...
But he is a symbol and a punctuation mark too, goddammit.
Trusted aide Kotomichi guards
the walls of his ward's consciousness.
His senses are surveillance equipment.
If someone suggests that the
Trade Minister is duplicitous
or that he is residing in the memory of another's life,
do not trust this person—
they could be an informant.
Trade Minister Tagomi knows that
every empire is a living thing with a grudge.
Every empire is asthmatic.
This one cringes at its own cruelty
but finds justification in every puddle.
The economic reasons for expansion are many
but few glisten with precarity
like the fetish for mined jewels,
or uranium.
Uranium is also in a constant state of decay.
The Trade Minister has an enclosure
of peace inside himself.
Kotomichi has the skeleton key to allow him entry.
Counselor Kellyanne Conway
does not struggle with lying—
it makes her giggle.
To herself, she repeats:
"The spoken word is always already
the betrayal of a silent truth.
The ripple restores stillness."

Trade Minister Tagomi's subversion
is stored in a shrine
composed of a photograph, fortune sticks,
and a banned book.
In her hands these objects will liquefy.
Some believe that Counselor Conway is a cipher
and that this very moment is a ruse,
shrouding another event.
So I have been punching walls
to see if they are facade.
I feel the pain but the blood
is also the Trade Minister's.
When I say out loud
"don't worry this regime will end soon,"
my voice sounds like a tape recording
of an old speech.

President Obama is in Town for the General Assembly

That poem is reticent to expose its argument:
Is it an intentional fragment?
Is it an aftershock
provoked by an imagined conflict
between the writer and her reader?

Surely it investigates epiphenomenon
almost impossible to trace.
But if the poem is only about poetry itself is it merely an event in language?
Does it skip stones
along the watery surface of expression
or to put it too bluntly dive its way into the deep?
Metaphors can be dangerous,
but they are not assault weapons.

Enough questions, at least for now.
Today I yearn for happenstance—
And I wait for a check from a freelance employer so I can pay some bills.
The September light is a paradox—
It shimmers yet produces
more shadow than ever before.
Perhaps it is the medication I'm on but I smell
peace in the autumn air.
Or maybe the apples that the boulevardiers are
biting have lent a scent.

My auntie once said:
"the pursuit of knowledge is a Sisyphean game.
Regardless one must play."
A physicist, she bragged that 96%
of the universe is not perceptible.
Trying to accept
that so much matter
and energy exists undetected
is a lesson in letting go.
No matter how early I rise I am always late for this class.

Pre-Existing Soliloquy

Non sequiturs stalk me.
They pounce at any pregnant pause
in my run-on consciousness.
Yes, I know it's all caps MY FAULT—
after all I did graduate work
in evasive studies …
and my research on the history
of the segue remains unpublished.
I just can't stay on topic,
except when I'm discussing
how I can't stay on topic:
then and only then
am I annoyingly repetitive.
As if you didn't know—
if I don't take my pill
I'll spend much too much time
pondering punctuation marks…
(I tend to bypass the semi-colon)
and sooner or later I'll slip
into a pre-existing soliloquy.

Express Mail

My mother used to say
some days no matter what you do the past arrives.
I imagined a package
filled with curling snapshots
sent express mail
by my Aunt from down south—
as if the past was stored below
the Mason-Dixon line.
Even up north
memory sometimes delivers
a return to sender story.
Without warning
lost and found images are superimposed atop
any and all perceptions of the moment.
When I was ten years old
I would have made those gin and tonics
for my mommy myself if she let me
(to make them weaker).
I can still hear the clink
of the ice cubes against the tumbler.
Two of them calmed her
but a third cocktail could unleash such frosty rage
that our southern-exposure home
began to shiver in the summer.
If only I could relive the joy
in overhearing her gossip with galpals
but my ability to repress ain't what it used to be.
The walls of that Jericho fell
one of the days that the past arrived.
Picture this:
the first time my mother
and I saw the Williams sisters
play tennis against each other—
a semi-final at Wimbledon in the year 2000.

I wanted younger sister Serena to kick ass.
Yet my mother articulated
Venus's dilemma to me—
she desires to win
but she needs to protect her baby sister.
My mother was almost bed-ridden by then but
didn't want anyone outside the family to know.
She had a sister
who was diagnosed with schizophrenia
and lived and died in Northern State Hospital
but my mother didn't want anyone
outside the family to know.
I watched my mother watch the match—
at times she was trying not to cry
but her cheeks yielded to a tear or two
after one long rally
and I realized
it was one of those days that the past arrives.

The House That Lota De Macedo Soares Built In Samambaia

A half-mile beyond where the bus
stopped struggling against
the slope of the mountain,
and past a hushed hamlet with one chatty café,
an unseen waterfall became the soundtrack
to the 3-D movie I confused with substance.
When the cascade was revealed
its babble was replaced by
the allegations of cotinga birds
and the pleas of tamarin monkeys.
Or so I imagine—
the source of these speech acts
was hidden from view.
Blue morpho butterflies with wings as large as
bandanas
swarmed like I was a rotting mango
as the mist shushed the fauna.
A few features of the morning
dominate my memory
and I overlook crucial details.
Even if this is the nature of remembrance
I apologize to the shapes
and colors and sounds and smells I omit.
At a bend of the road
across the ravine—
I recognized the tableau vivant
from photographs and descriptions.
But the monologue of the bigwig at the café—
like a voice-over in a film noir—
returned to me.
I translate:
"Do not walk onto the property—
the owner will have you arrested…or worse…
she'll shoot you."

At least I imagine
this was his warning as he spoke so fast...
Admittedly I do have the gene for hyperbole.
I walked to the gate
and hugged the soggy view:
My camera reproduced
only a faint outline
of the mid-century assemblage
so memory alone stores the perspective.
My dizziness subsided
as I realized what was in front of me:
the house that Lota de Macedo Soares
built in Samambaia.

The Triumvirate

The Poet perceives the symmetry of thorn and calyx.
The garishness of rose petals is intolerable
And nothing competes
with the blueprints of his beloved.
In a land that finds solace in ostentation
The Emperor attempts to balance
idealism and resignation
by enforcing laws and levying taxes.
But he just can't stop eating Sacher Torte.
Slumped against the triumphal arch
the eyes of the Poet wring out the rain.
the Viennese widow conducts her guests
with a baton made of manners and wit.
Still she craves a letter most.
A scented document to lock away
in a Koloman Moser desk.
The Emperor foresees how trickery
and subterfuge design the horizon.
The people's need to conquer chaos
is now the quieting of the scream inside his head.
Make no mistake. The Emperor has gone mad
and so the border must be sealed
against imaginary Ottomans.
The Poet will never realize that simplicity
is not the antidote to lavishness.
He writes to a woman
who refuses him
entrance to her famed residence
inside the Ringstrasse.
Nonetheless her beauty encloses him
like a gondola of the giant Ferris Wheel at the Prater.

Rumi's Stipend

Is there a financier ready to cut a check
When you finally become
Conscious of consciousness?
Dream on pal.

Even when you
Surpass the limitations of your thoughts
Rent is still due dude.
There is no per diem for the wise.
Chant a sacred syllable
Or practice deep listening all you want—
Your deadline remains a fact not an illusion.
A year-end bonus for enlightenment
(or transcendence)?
Fat chance bro.

Ah, but surely
Storming the gates of selfhood
Is itself a victory…
And maybe, you guys, there is a genius grant
For those who neither indulge
In endless neediness
Nor cry me me me!

But kiddo there just ain't no such thing.
Don't worry:
Some schmuck—invoice in hand—
Will appear miraculously
And announce that you must build your brand.

The Warning

During the waxing of the sturgeon moon the bay stretches and contracts with ever-increasing drama. Last night I could swear a spotlight atop the seabed illuminated the sky. Checking my bank account online this morning forced me to tally all the bills still to pay. Later I surrendered to the vista. When I rounded the bend on the beach a colony of seals ignored me. Surely there is value in hearing a pinniped bark with a sense of entitlement that is neither *nouveau* nor ancestral. Back home, the age-related changes to my skin made me crave a new anti-anxiety med…or a miraculous anti-wrinkle cream. I yearned for the immaculate, scrubbed all surfaces, hid the clutter, and arranged wildflowers in quirky vases from the swap shop.

Warning: Arriving means his departure is inevitable.

When you are here every utterance churns up an issue that then must be resolved (when you say this, I feel that…). O strike me dead now, while I teeter on the edge of giggling ceaselessly at the inanity of relationships. Must I confess to my own imprudence? Must I alternate between strategic forgetting and deliberate forgiving? Past some dusty crossroad, my personality becomes a penitentiary.

Warning: Do not have "a relationship talk" in this zip code. Best to transfer all discord onto decisions about dinner. Study the patterns: the contours of the wiggly dune; the trajectory of the fatso seagull; the tracks the jeep's tire leaves in the sand. The big picture is redundant pointillism.

*I might argue with him now...but when he leaves,
I will crave his close-up and yearn for his comical
whine. Arriving means his departure is inevitable.*

Surely the bobbing head of a seal in the whitecaps matters more than any utterance calculated to explain my behavior. The retreat to low tide leaves behind sea lettuce, mermaid's hair, and yes, horseshoe crabs—confirmation of a crime of indulgence cheered on by the swell of the moon. Coupled with the wind these events will accumulate into something like a dune, but also a mistrust fund consisting of assets from inevitable nor'easters. This makeshift cliff is ready to collapse: The sea will reclaim its property. If poems are also evidentiary, why have I failed to convince? I still yearn for the immaculate. I'd rather be fanciful than obvious though I'm not sure I can afford it right now. At the end of the day, gesture tickles words into relevance. And the mute deer ticks have clearly made their point. I have driftwood to collect and loans to pay back. If you go, you miss the blooming of the coneflowers.

Two Coins and Three Stanzas

On Tuesdays the library is closed until 2pm.
I waited, ready to pounce on the clock
like an ambush predator.
Sunning on the table outside lay two quarters.
50 cents equals ten minutes in the dryer
or 30 at the parking meter by the hardware store.
Time itself is not legal tender
but coins are somehow also minutes…
And free money—like the lottery
or an unexpected inheritance—
always corrects an injustice of some sort.
But I let the coins be.

The elderly couple at the corner
proudly refuse charity from their
wealthy washashore neighbors.
Instead they accept canned goods
from the church's food pantry.
(Imagine the bidding war
if they put their charming craftsman's cottage
on the market!)
The couple read to each other
from large print books.
Once I noticed the librarians
exchanging looks of concern—

I've probably stared at them
too long myself.
Surely an elder is not a foreigner
in a fishing village
that has become
too fashionable for its own good.
Not everyone wants to go to Florida
or can afford Costa Rica upon retirement.
Plus it is rude to gape like a landed fish.

That evening we barbecued turkey burgers
and seared fresh tuna.
A fox appeared,
remnants of winter coat on its slim body,
looking mangy and underfed.
Their population has grown
and though I know they are omnivores
I worry there is not enough rodents left
for the kits to hunt.
All the conservationists advise
do not feed the wildlife
but it is not easy to avert hunger's eagle eyes.

The Moment and the Sequence

Droplets of the bay on his lashes,
high tide rollicking about his shoulders.
His face soft and wet, almost weary,
almost refreshed,
plump rosy lips slightly parted,
seemingly ready for a kiss,
curly dark hair cascading down his forehead.
I caught him staring at me
as I dove under the surface
wanting to show him
how I could do handstands underwater.
Silly me.
I took his look to be a statement:
"What love I feel for him!"

Years later, I realized
that his gaze had another message:
"I am sad that I am going to leave him.
 How bittersweet is this moment."

His propensity for unfaithfulness was once again
revealing itself with a fellow
he met while drunk at
the aptly named bar, *The Monster*—
just as he was drunk
when I introduced myself on the dance floor
after he danced close to me
and then encircled me with endearing,
sloppy desire.
Now I know when they met
and now I know when we broke up.

He felt guilty and happy
(not weary not refreshed)
as he was falling in love with another.
And I was in denial, a voice inside me repeated:
"Yes, yes he is still the one for me.
I can remake him. He can remake me.
And our remade selves can be together forever." Ha!

If only I could have stayed
afloat during the sequence
rather than diving into the moment over and over.

Yesterday I Had the Hiccups

I am allergic to being ignored.
Please scratch my itches
before I tip-toe
back and forth along the bluff
and find delight in
my own compulsion to repeat.
It is a sure bet I'll retaliate
and grouse a regrettable phase.
Down the fire road on the left,
where the horse flies lie in wait,
one's personality is downgraded
to a debtor's prison.

After all is said and done,
there is still more to do.
Events jolt:
they overawe all patterns,
only to be "processed,"
squeezed into a jack in the box.
We have therapy to thank for that.
A speech act is also a hiccup.
And vice versa, my darling.

I mime Sisyphus—
A voice told me that somewhere uphill
I might find an antidote
to the venom in your wordlessness.

Edward D. Miller was born in Brooklyn, NY. He lives now in Cape Cod with his husband and a Chatterdale (Chihuahua mixed with Patterdale Terrier). He teaches film, media, and performance at the College of Staten Island and the Graduate Center of the City University of New York. He writes creative nonfiction as well as poetry.

www.ingramcontent.com/pod-product-compliance
Lightning Source LLC
LaVergne TN
LVHW041509070426
835507LV00012B/1437